Introduction to Plant

**The Essential Guide to Plant Propagation
Methods and Techniques**

Gardening Series
Dueep Jyot Singh
Mendon Cottage Books

JD-Biz Publishing

Disclaimer

The information is this book is provided for informational purposes only. It is not intended to be used and medical advice or a substitute for proper medical treatment by a qualified health care provider. The information is believed to be accurate as presented based on research by the author.

The contents have not been evaluated by the U.S. Food and Drug Administration or any other Government or Health Organization and the contents in this book are not to be used to treat cure or prevent disease.

The author or publisher is not responsible for the use or safety of any diet, procedure or treatment mentioned in this book. The author or publisher is not responsible for errors or omissions that may exist.

Warning

The Book is for informational purposes only and before taking on any diet, treatment or medical procedure, it is recommended to consult with your primary health care provider.

Our books are available at

1. Amazon.com
2. Barnes and Noble
3. Itunes
4. Kobo
5. Smashwords
6. Google Play Books

Table of Contents

Introduction

\It is always been the nature of human beings to try to improve on nature. That is why, you can be certain that millenniums ago when some enterprising soul learned how to domesticate wild plants and grow them in his own little yard for food, shelter and wood, one fine day he decided – what is going to happen if I can grow the branch of such and such tree on such and such other tree? That means I am going to have oranges and apples in one parent tree.

The start of such creative ideas must have given rise to many bizarre experimentations, most of which would fail monumentally. However, as time went by, and more and more people started to experiment, they gained more knowledge and gardening experience related to plant propagation.

In the natural state, you are going to see different vegetative propagation methods through which a plant can grow. That means the plant is going to grow its own seeds, and use natural methods like air, wind and water to spread the seeds far and wide.

In a strawberry, you are going to have the plant sending out long branches trailing on the soil. Stimulus of moisture causes the production of roots below a bud on a long branch. The bud is then going to send out shoots. Soon the connection between the new plant and the old plant is severed by a withering up of the intervening branch.

In the same way, the Agave – which we also know as aloe – produces a tall pole on which small bulbils grow. These are going to fall off and each would usually produce roots, which will then grow into new plants.

Each plant bulb that you see is just a potentially germinating bud packed up in food material.

In the case of Bryophyllum, you are going to have a leaf that can be planted and it is going to bring forth shoots.

So that means just one leaf would be capable of populating the whole forest with Bryophyllum plants!

All these natural propagation methods should show you how nature manages to keep plants surviving under adverse conditions. The survival instinct of plants is very highly developed. That is why they have managed to adapt themselves to different environments, atmospheres, and conditions.

The natural propagation methods used for propagating baby plants in Bryophyllum were noted by gardeners, ages ago, and they decided to try that same experiment on Begonia. Begonia could also be grown through leaf cuttings.

The natural propagation of strawberries was repeated and tried out in the artificial layering of climbers climbing up all over our walls, balconies, arbors and pergolas.

In the same way, we looked at the way the agave grew, and thus learned about cuttings to grow many other varieties of plants.

So now we are going to learn about the various methods of plant propagation, which we can utilize to grow many types of plants in our garden. All of these methods have been time tested, and have been in use for centuries, throughout the world. In the 21st century we may be using technical shortcuts for growing plants with artificial lighting and harmful hormones, but the basic rules of gardening apply universally.

So this book is going to tell you more about how natural gardening plant propagation techniques are being used even today to create richer harvests, and also unusual cultivars.

Layering

Compared to cuttings, layering is a plant propagation process which has been overlooked by a number of gardeners. That is because layering is slower, even though it is surer than other propagation processes.

In layering, you are not going to interrupt the supply food and water from the mother to what is going to be a new plant. However, in cuttings, the new plant-to-be is cut off entirely from the mother plant and it has to depend on its own food and water contained in itself or taken from the soil. In this respect, the plants that we call soft wooded with succulent tissues are going to have more advantage over so-called hard wooded plants which comparatively do not have large stores of water in them.

As I said before propagation by layering is a comparatively slower process, even if it is more sure. Larger and more advanced plants can be obtained by layers than by cuttings.

So how do you start layering your plants? First of all you are going to select the branch of wood which has to be layered. This wood should be sturdy enough to bear being bent down to the earth without breaking.

Now cut the branch half through with a sharp knife, just under one of the leaf buds towards its extremity. Then pass the knife upward so as to slit the branch about an inch or two up.

This slit piece with the leaf bud at its extremity is called a *tongue*.

It should be kept open by inserting a small piece of tile or a match in the cutting. Remove the earth to the depth of two or 3 inches from, or place a flower pot over the spot just with the tongue falls on the branch being bent down. Then carefully bend the tongue portion of the branch into the earth or into your flowerpot.

Secure it in that position by a peg. Now, cover it with soil or earth which should be pressed down, and watered.

If you are doing the layering in the month of February or March, it is very essential that the soil should be frequently watered. Layering is best done in roses, when you are going to have the tongue at the upper part of the shoot. That means it should not be in the part which forms the bough.

It should also be within 2 inches of the surface, so as to feel the effects of the heat in the atmosphere. If this is not done properly, you are not going to get speedy rooting.

There is another way in which layering can be done, which can be practiced extensively in roses. And also in other plants where the boughs are really rigid and do not bend down easily, you can try this layering method.

Get a flowerpot which has part of its side broken and make a tongue in the branch which you need to layer. Raise the flowerpot up so that the branch passing through the broken side can have the tongue part at just about 2 inches below the level of the soil, when the pot is filled in

Keep the flowerpot permanently in this position by some support placed beneath it. Insert a piece of tile in the pot, where the pot side is broken away and then fill the pot with a mellow soil composed of leaf mold and sand. This potted soil should be kept moist constantly.

Here is a URL where you are going to find extremely good instructional steps on how you can layer a plant according to the instructions given above. Of course, a flowerpot has not been used to support the plant in the initial stages, but then you can use a flowerpot as and when you like or think it necessary.

http://www.wikihow.com/Cut-and-Layer-Plants

How long is it going to take for the roots to grow? The time it takes for the roots to be found from the cut surface in the pot may to some extent be seen by the vigor of the growth of the part beyond the cut.

It is sensible to leave the layer intact for about two months. After that, gradually sever the connection of the layer with the parent plant. This is going to be done by cutting a small notch in the branch between the pot on the parent plant and deepening it every second day, it is going to take a fortnight to separate the plant completely.

For layering any sort of herbaceous plant, which roots quickly, like let us say a carnation, these were the gardening tactics used in Royal Gardens in France, about 200 years ago. A piece of oiled paper was folded around the stem to be layered. This would form a funnel. This paper could be then held together with pins or any other holding material.

Soil was then inserted into this funnel, along with Moss. The moss at the mouth of the funnel would retain all of the moisture and thus encourage new plant growth.

You can also have small four-inch pots divided into halves vertically, like tiles. Pass the branch which you need to layer through these and tie together firmly. Fill the pot up with good soil. Continue watering regularly and in six months or so, you are going to have new plants. This process is known in America as *"Marcottee."*

Marcottee

This is a popular mode of plant propagation in which you are going to select a firm and healthy branch of a plant. The wood should be well ripened. Take off a small ring of bark under a leaf bud. This should be about 1 inch wide.

Scrape the woody part, well so that no bark remains.

Now apply a ball of well-tempered clay. Bind it on secure with soft binding, tow or a bandage.

You can make it fast to a stake, if necessary. Hang a small pot having a hole in the bottom just over the Marcotee. Supply it with water daily. In a few months, you are going to have a fine and well rooted new plant.

As more and more growth is emitted from the bud that is above the "wound" the fibers are going to descend into the ball of earth and form roots.

As soon as they are seen coming out through the bandage, your branch can be cut off from the parent tree. This cutting should be done progressively, as advised above – in the layering section.

After this the new plant can be planted in the place where it is intended to remain.

This is how you are going to get strong and well rooted plants. You can also acquire duplicates of desirable plants through this process.

Any Marcotti made in June is going to be well rooted in October. On the other hand, of the 45 layers made in June on the same individual tree, it is still going to take the time for the rooting to start. The Chinese Litchie requires four months to form good roots. You can also use it successfully for citrus fruits.

Here is the traditional way in which the Marcottee is still made in many parts of the world.

Eastern Rope Trick

A piece of rope has a knot tied to one end of it. The other end is passed through a securely hanging pot and drawn through the hole at the bottom until the knot is brought down to fall upon and close up the hole.

This rope is now secure. That is because the knotted end is inside the pot. Now it is carried on to its full extent and coiled around the mud and earth.

By this means, the water, which when poured into the pot, is going to trickle out slowly. It is then going to go down the rope, and thus onto the soil, keeping it moist. This water is thus distributed to the whole soil bundle.

This also prevents the water in the pot from flowing out too fast. Very often it is not going to fall upon the soil package at all. So use the rope trick to provide water to your future new plant.

The bark has been removed from a piece of branch, before the moist earth is bandaged around it.

Cuttings

There are some plants which can be propagated by cuttings at nearly all times of the year. On the other hand, there are plants, which grow only in one particular season – that of the most vigorous growth. For example, Verbena cuttings are made most successfully in the cold season, but Stephanotis grows best during the rains.

Some cuttings are going to strike so readily that you do not have to worry about how you are going to put them in the ground. On the other hand, other cuttings are going to strike even better if you insert them sloping wise into the ground. They may not give you the best results if you just plant them upright.

When you are laying out the cuttings sloping wise, there submits should not be more than an inch higher above the ground. The earth should be able to cover all but the two uppermost buds.

The cuttings thus protected are not going to dry up. The rooting end is also going to be better aerated.

The end of the cutting which is to be inserted in the soil should be cut across with a clean-cut, just below a leaf bud.

You can make slips instead of cuttings. A slip is a small shoot which is pulled off a plant at the point of junction with the stem, bringing away with it a piece of wood and bark from the stem.

None of the leaves or as few as possible should be removed from the upper end of a cutting.

The age and the condition of the wood from where these cuttings are most suitably taken is going to depend on the nature of the plant.

This is where you are going to use your own experience or ask the guidance and advice of a more experienced gardener. For example, cuttings of a young and tender wood can propagate to the plant of Inga freely.

When the wood begins to assume a brownish color, or is half opened, just like in just like in Passiflora or Bauhinia, you can begin to propagate cuttings from it. Some plants only "strike" freely when the wood is perfectly ripe. These include roses and Vitis [grapes.]

Now let us take the example of strawberry. You are going to have two kinds of branches here. One ascends and the other branches along the ground like runners. You are going to use the lower trailing shoots for propagation. These are going to form plants. In the same way, suckers can also form plants.

Strawberry runners can produce plants through attaching themselves to the soil and setting up roots there.

Cuttings of the upper shoots are going to produce flowering laterals in a very short time. That is how blooming specimens can be raised in one season by taking off the extremities of the longest shoots and using them as cuttings.

In fact, these pruning of the shoots were responsible for early blooming of plants and the regulation of plant growth, in the 18th and 19th centuries. This regulation was done by the distance at which the cutting was taken from the main stem.

"Striking" Cuttings Successfully

When you are trying to propagate a plant through cuttings, your main priority is to see that you maintain a proper water supply to the cutting. That is, so that it can absorb nutrients for itself. This is going to promote the development of the shoot. It is also going to secure the proper and adequate aeration of the rooted end of the cutting.

A large number of the plants can be raised from cutting which have been laid down in common garden soil. This is normally done in wet weather in an open situation without shelter, either from the sun or from the wet weather.

The location is thus going to be exposed to the full action of the atmosphere and this is the best for your plants. That is because your new cuttings definitely cannot bear sour earth, which normally occurs during the wet weather in situations which are sheltered and secluded without any exposure to air, and the sun.

Here is the best way in which you can propagate your favorite kinds of plants, by just using these easy to implement this.

Using Sand

This sand is excellent in which to plant cuttings.

Cuttings of plants put down in the open ground are not going to succeed. However, they can grow well in sand. This is how you are going to start your cuttings growing.

Take a small piece of ground, in an open situation. Enclose it around with a wall one – two feet high. You are now going to fill this enclosure with the finest sand procurable. Now insert the cuttings in the sand, water them well and press them down. You can also cover with Bell glasses, if the weather seems to be harsh or cold. Shade with a roof of matting, fixed about 2 feet above them.

These glasses are going to be taken off more than once or twice weekly, so that you can water the cutting. Keep doing this so that the cuttings are clean of any decayed matter or leaves which may cause fungal growth due to moisture on the glass surface of the Bell glasses.

Another modification of this particular plan is to fill small pots with sand, with the cuttings close around the inside of them. Now sink the pots to the brim in a bed of sand and covered them with Bell glasses.

When the cuttings take hold [strike], the pots may be taken out and other pots with fresh cuttings can be fitted in their places. Consider the sand to be your long-term incubator. In this way, when the cuttings are removed, the bed of sand is not going to be disturbed as it would have been if the pots had not been employed.

You can try any other means available with the same results. For example, in point of convenience, you can sink the pots of sand with the cuttings in them in a suitable corner of your garden and cover it with Bell glasses for shading.

Here is another simplest modification – I am giving you three choices, for your own benefit! – And all of these methods have been used down the ages, and are time tested.

Fill a flower pot half full of sand, insert the cuttings of length sufficient to reach, within a little, the rim of the pot. Sink the pot in the earth and cover with a pane of glass. Each morning the underside of the glass is going to be covered with condensed moisture. All you have to do is to turn it upside down!

So like I said if you do not have Bell glass, use a glass pane!

Why do you need to sink the pots to the rim? That is because when you are striking cuttings, the soil in which they are inserted should be of a somewhat higher temperature than the surrounding atmosphere. You are going to get that from sand. On the other hand, if you leave the pots above ground, evaporation is going to take place, from the porous sides of the pot. This is going to reduce the temperature of the soil within them. So the cuttings are not going to get a good chance for striking properly.

In many parts of the East, these strikings are normally done even today with three parts of sand and one part of fine charcoal. That is because the availability of charcoal in these particular areas is quite easy, and nobody's bothered much about global warming, due to its production.

Also, I found some really innovative people who could not afford Bell glasses, which were not easily available in their particular areas, making do with the glasses from glass lanterns! That is, of course, in a place where glass lanterns are still very much in use. Even four sided bulb shades, which had been discarded because they had been cracked, can be used as stylish Bell jars.

Make sure the glass jar has a glass roof. A tin or a metal roof is going to heat up the atmosphere within the enclosed space.

Traditional Cutting Growing Technique

All right, you say you do not have any empty and spare place in your garden in which you can grow these cuttings. In this time and age, where sustainable gardening is the norm of the day, and every little bit of land is being put in use, you can grow cuttings in a shallow pan.

This is something I saw done, in a nursery garden, about two decades ago, and I just recalled it. So if you are strapped for space, you do not have to worry about where to strike your cuttings.

Get a wide and shallow planting pan, [this is going to have a hole in the bottom for drainage purposes] and lay at the bottom of it a large quantity of potsherds, broken bricks, crocks, etc. for drainage purposes. I will be showing you an illustration of a cross-section of this particular pan so that you can see what needs to be done, further down.

Over the drainage, near the circumference, you are going to put a layer of equal parts of leaf compost and mold and sand. Now you are going to fill the plant to within half an inch of the rim with pure sand.

Now put in the cuttings with their bases against the side of the pan. They should be just above the mixture of leaf mold and sloping. That means their summits are going to project out of the sand in a small circle in the center of the pan.

Then you can put down the Bell glass or the Hand glass just large enough to enclose the circle of leafy ends.

Sink the pan to its rim in the earth in some shady place, and water the sand outside the hand glass daily.

Place a piece of matting over the whole at night to prevent the effect of cold from radiation. This is going to be injurious to your young plant.

Cross-section of the container pan with cuttings striking with new growth.

The bottom layer is made up of pebbles and leaf compost, covered with sand. The shallow pan has been sunk in ordinary soil in your garden.

Benefits of Shallow Pan Technique

Here are some benefits, which have a clear advantage over other cutting propagation techniques.

The bases of the cuttings are laid against a support – against the side of the pot or the pan. Remember that direction is slanting, and the cuttings have to be in the sandy portion.

As they are laid sloping, the cuttings are well covered from the air without their lower ends being too deep in the sand.

You do not need to take off the glass, until the cuttings have struck.

The pan being sunk in the ground means that there is no effect of the cold through incorporation from its outer side.

If you do not have a Bell glass, or a hand glass, you can try another method.

Triple Pot Method

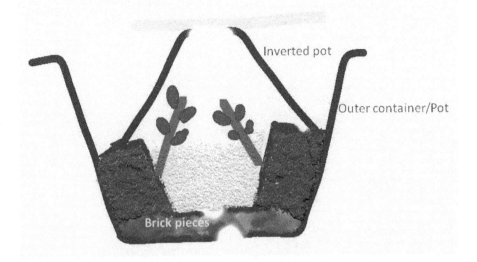

Take a large flower pot. Lay at the bottom of it, large loose pieces of brick just so high that a small flower pot placed inside and upon them can have its rim on the same level as the rim of the larger pot.

Fill in the empty spaces between both the pots with perfectly fine sand or earth. Fill the inner part with pure sand, and insert the cuttings.

Take another pot just of the size that, when turned upside down, it may fit in on the earth between the rims of the large pot and the small pot.

Break the bottom portion of the upturned pot and cover it with a piece of window glass.

Water the cuttings when they require it with lukewarm water, allowing none to fall on the earth between the pots.

When condensation takes place upon the pane of glass, just turn it over. The object is to keep the earth between the pots dry. This is so that no evaporation may take place from the outside of the large pot and the temperature within can be reduced.

Propagation through Buds

Propagation through buds is a very popular method of propagation, especially in the matter of grapevines.

The method of this propagation is simply to take a plump shoot on which the leaves are healthy and the buds have not yet started. About half an inch or less above and below a bud, you cut the shoot sloping wise into the wood.

The cut each way is going to be just about a quarter of an inch behind the bud. This piece of the shoot with the bud upon it just as it is, is now going to be planted firmly in a pan of sand. The point of the bud is just going to be visible above the surface.

Make sure that the bud has the leaf attached to it which should not be taken off. This method of propagation is excellent for citrus fruits, and Camellias and roses.

Cutting a Bud from a Branch

Budded plants are more free in their growth and thus they are more prolific. You can perform this budding on any shoot of a full-grown plant if all the branches, except the budding ones are cut away. On the other hand, I would advise to raise seedlings or in the case of roses, make cuttings expressly for the purpose of budding upon.

Seedlings of most plants are going to be ready for the purpose in about 12 months from the time the seed has been sown. Make sure the seedlings are transplanted previous to the budding operation, either on the spot where they are going to remain permanently or elsewhere. They should also be thoroughly established before you try budding on them.

Budding is normally performed at two seasons of the year – when the plants are about to start for their spring growth and again when they are ready to begin their Midsummer growth. This is the time when the bark separates, most freely from the wood.

For the operation of budding you need a ball of cotton twist thread, a sharp knife and a budding knife.

You can easily make a budding knife by filing a thin piece of bamboo into the form and size of a Lancet and fix it in a wooden handle.

Now check the condition of the plant. Can it be used as a stock plant? It should be fit and healthy.

Now make a cut through the bark down upon the wood. See whether the budding knife can be thrust freely between the bark and the wood. If the bark adheres firmly, which means that you can only raise it by tearing it away, it is going to be of no use for budding purposes. On the other hand, if the bark is found to yield readily the operation can be commenced safely.

Make a gash through the bark across the branch in the place where you are going to do the budding. From the center of the gash, make another gash about an inch and a half downwards.

Making gashes in the branch.

The bud is now going to be inserted after you have taken it from the branch on which it is growing. The bud should be plump and if it has a leaf growing beneath it, cut the leaf off. That means you are left about with about a quarter of an inch of the stalk adhering below the bud.

Preparing a bud

Then pass your knife into the branch about half an inch above the bud sliced down a thin piece of the wood with the bark and with the bud still upon it.

Bring the knife out at about two thirds of an inch below the bud. The bark with the bud is now going to be called the "Shield."

Before inserting it, it is desirable that the wood adhering to it has to be removed. That is going to take a little bit of care, so that you do not injure the bud.

This is how you are going to do it. Hold the Shield in the left hand and thrusting the thumbnail of the right hand between the wood and the bark off the upper part of the Shield, remove the wood from the bark by pulling it off downwards.

Make sure that the bark is kept inflexible and erect all this while. By adopting this method, a little wood may be left behind, but there is absolutely no fear of the bud being damaged.

If you find this procedure troublesome, do not worry, it is not essential to do that. Some gardeners never do it. Some even condemned this practice. According to them, they say that the wood assists in keeping the bud moist and prevents it from being destroyed by the heat. They may be possibly right.

They also say, by inserting the bud, just as it is cut from the Shield, the operation of budding is going to be far more easy, more speedy and is going to be equally successful.

As soon after the Shield is ready, you must lift up on the longitudinal gash which you made in the branch previously with the budding knife.

 The Shield is then going to be slipped down so as to lie upon the naked wood of the branch similarly situated as it was upon the branch from which it was taken.

Now cut half the part of the Shield off, that is above the Bud with a crosscut. That means the upper part of the Shield is going to lie close and even against the crosscut of the branch.

Inserting the bud into the branch gash.

Bind the whole firmly but not tightly with cotton twist. In the East, jute fiber and coconut fiber is also used as a natural binding thread. The bud is now going to remain exposed.

The first indication of the bud having taken is going to be the falling off of the little bit of leaf stalk which was left adhering to it.

When the bud has put forth about a quarter of an inch of growth, you should remove the cotton binding, but do not disturb the branch until the bud has sent forth a considerable shoot.

It has been found that the wood containing buds by packing them carefully in moist moss and even sawdust are going to last for a long time. That is how citrus buds and rose buds have been sent all over the world to nurseries abroad or even in the country for years.

The whole budding process can be seen on this excellent URL.

http://www.wikihow.com/Do-Budding-in-Plants

Grafting

Grafting is the art of uniting one part of one plant to another plant, which is going to nourish it. The part which is united is called the *graft or the scion.* The plant, which nourishes it, after the union has been done, is called the *stock.*

How long mankind has known about this process, can be seen in the Holy Bible, when St. Paul spoke of the grafting of the wild olive tree onto the good olive tree. [Romans XI, 17 – 24.] This simile is however inverted in general practice. The grafting is going to be done of a good scion onto a wild tree.

Benefits

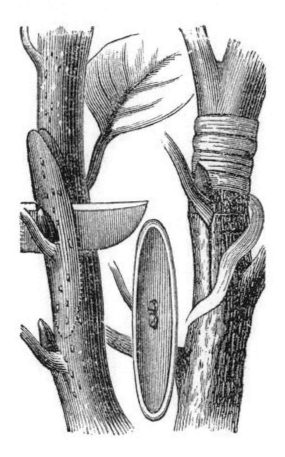

Here are the benefits of grafting.

Firstly, you can change the character of an existing tree. You are also going to propagate the plant, which may not grow certainly from cuttings or from seeds.

Grafting can get you dwarf trees and trees which are going to give you heavily bearing harvests.

Grafting also means that fruiting is quicker and plants are multiplied rapidly.

The stock and the scion are going to influence each other. That means one variety of citrus fruits can be grown on a stock plant of another citrus fruit variety successfully.

Grafting can only be done between allied varieties and species of plants, you cannot graft an orange scion on the stock of a mango and vice versa. However, you can graft the lime scion on an orange stock, and vice versa.

The most important grafting methods followed traditionally are given below.

Wedge Grafting

For this the scion and the stock must be nearly of the same thickness and age. Select a vigorous stock. "Head" it to within about six – 8 inches of the soil. Cut it cleanly with a sharp knife.

Then get the scion and cut it into the stock firmly. It is going to be quite sufficient if one side only fits in the square. But take care never to separate the scion and the stock after they have been fixed. If that happens, the graft is not going to be a success.

Having fixed the stock and the scion, tie the junction firmly with cotton bandages or you can smear over with the grafting wax, the recipe of which is given below.

In many parts of Asia, when they did not know about grafting wax which is the European gardening technique, the smearing was done with fresh cow dung and garden soil. Well, this is good to protect the plant, while giving it nourishment at the same time.

Keep the graft in the shade, because too much sun is going to wither it. This graft is going to be established within six weeks and give you a healthy plant.

Other grafting methods can be seen on this URL –
http://www.ag.ndsu.edu/hort/info/fruit/graft/graft.htm

Grafting Wax Solutions

Melt together equal parts of bees wax and resin. As this is an inflammable mixture, do this over a water bath. Allow to cool until it can be touched with the fingers and then to every 2 pounds of this mixture Add 1 pint of alcohol. Mix well and put up in tightly corked bottles. Apply with a brush.

Grafting Wax

Heat together 6 pounds of resin, 2 pounds of beeswax, and 1 pint of linseed oil over a water bath. Stir well, allow cooling and then preserve in a jar. When you want a wax to smear upon a union, this is extremely useful. But remember to dip your hands in linseed oil, before you use this wax for joining the unions.

Other grafting methods can be seen on this URL –

http://www.ag.ndsu.edu/hort/info/fruit/graft/graft.htm

Conclusion

This book has given you lots of information about plant propagation, and the best way in which you can grow plants from other plants, in we can almost say cloning vegetative methods.

Here are some more URLs which I have found useful, and you may want to look at them, for different ways of propagation.

Growing Cuttings in Water

http://www.motherearthliving.com/gardening/water-works.aspx.

The author of this particular blog has tried growing herbs in water. In one issue of the Popular Gardeners Chronicle, written somewhere in the 19th century, the process was to tie bottles by the neck and hang them in the windows of a small greenhouse[1] having filled them with clean water.

 The gardener then put in slips of Salvia or anything else, he wished to propagate, especially herbs. In about two or three weeks or a month, silver like roots appear and in a week or 10 days, the gardener could plant them in small pots well – watered. These plants never seemed to mind the change.

The cuttings should all be of Green wood, taking during the full growing season. Such settings are not going to flag during a hot summer.

When fibrous shoots appear about the base, transfer to any light soil. Balsam and Dahlias can be propagated freely in water, as well as plants belonging to the Melon family. These plants are formed in a very short period, just say

---

[1] At that time, greenhouses were very common, but I would say any sunny window.

about three days and when you transfer them to small pots, full of a natural leaf mold, you are going to have perfect balls of roots in less than a week.

Points for Water Cuttings

Here are some points which you want to keep in mind, when you are doing water cuttings. The bottle should be capacious, so that there is less likelihood of the water becoming foul. The water should be changed often to ensure it being fresh and pure.

The water when changing should be lukewarm, so as to afford in some degree to provide the plant with "bottom heat" which is so necessary for the speedy transformation of the roots and "callus".

The cuttings should be taken from the summit of the youngest shoot in a state of vigorous growth at the time of removal.

The cuttings should be sheltered from the wind and the sun otherwise without the proper amount of air and light, they are going to grow in a stunted fashion.

They should be removed out of the cold air, and taken into your house at night. You can also plunge the bottles half way up in a lukewarm bath, so that your plants can keep warm in harsh and cold weather.

So, allow your garden to flourish with all these plant propagation methods which have been in use for centuries all over the world.

Live Long and Prosper!

Author Bio

Dueep Jyot Singh is a Management and IT Professional who managed to gather Postgraduate qualifications in Management and English and Degrees in Science, French and Education while pursuing different enjoyable career options like being an hospital administrator, IT,SEO and HRD Database Manager/ trainer, movie , radio and TV scriptwriter, theatre artiste and public speaker, lecturer in French, Marketing and Advertising, ex-Editor of Hearts On Fire (now known as Solstice) Books Missouri USA, advice columnist and cartoonist, publisher and Aviation School trainer, ex-moderator on Medico.in, banker, student councilor ,travelogue writer … among other things!

One fine morning, she decided that she had enough of killing herself by Degrees and went back to her first love -- writing. It's more enjoyable! She already has 48 published academic and 14 fiction- in- different- genre books under her belt.

When she is not designing websites or making Graphic design illustrations for clients , she is browsing through old bookshops hunting for treasures, of which she has an enviable collection – including R.L. Stevenson, O.Henry, Dornford Yates, Maurice Walsh, De Maupassant, Victor Hugo, Sapper, C.N. Williamson, "Bartimeus" and the crown of her collection- Dickens "The Old Curiosity Shop," and so on… Just call her "Renaissance Woman") - collecting herbal remedies, acting like Universal Helping Hand/Agony Aunt, or escaping to her dear mountains for a bit of exploring, collecting herbs and plants and trekking.

Check out some of the other JD-Biz Publishing books

THE MAGIC OF GOOSEBERRIES FOR HEALTH AND BEAUTY
Natural Remedy Series
JD-Biz Publishing
Dueep J Singh and John Davidson

THE MAGIC OF YOGURT FOR COOKING AND BEAUTY
Natural Remedy Series
JD-Biz Publishing
Dueep J Singh and John Davidson

THE MAGIC OF LEMONS USING LEMONS FOR HEALTH AND BEAUTY
Natural Remedy Series
JD-Biz Publishing
Dueep J Singh and John Davidson

THE MAGIC OF CHILLIES FOR COOKING AND HEALING
Natural Remedy Series
JD-Biz Publishing
Dueep J Singh and John Davidson

THE MAGIC OF ONIONS ONIONS IN CUISINE TO CURE AND TO HEAL
Natural Remedy Series
JD-Biz Publishing
Dueep J Singh and John Davidson

THE MAGIC OF RADISHES TO CURE AND TO HEAL
Natural Remedy Series
JD-Biz Publishing
Dueep J Singh and John Davidson

THE MAGIC OF CARROTS TO CURE AND TO HEAL
Natural Remedy Series
JD-Biz Publishing
Dueep J Singh and John Davidson

THE HEALTH BENEFITS OF OREGANO FOR COOKING AND HEALTH
Natural Remedy Series
JD-Biz Publishing
M. Usman and John Davidson

The Magic Of MARIGOLDS Marigolds for Health And Beauty
Natural Remedy Series
JD-Biz Publishing
Dueep J Singh and John Davidson

THE HEALTH BENEFITS OF CINNAMON
Natural Remedy Series
JD-Biz Publishing
M. Usman and J. Davidson

THE MAGIC OF COCONUTS FOR COOKING & HEALTH
Health Learning Series
JD-Biz Publishing
Dueep J Singh and John Davidson

THE MAGIC OF CLOVES FOR HEALING AND COOKING
Health Learning Series
JD-Biz Publishing
Dueep J Singh and John Davidson

THE MAGIC OF ASAFETIDA FOR COOKING AND HEALING
Health Learning Series
JD-Biz Publishing
Dueep J Singh and John Davidson

THE MAGIC OF NEEM MARGOSA TO HEAL
Natural Remedy Series
JD-Biz Publishing
Dueep J Singh and John Davidson

THE MAGIC OF SALT TO HEAL AND FOR BEAUTY
Natural Remedy Series
JD-Biz Publishing
Dueep J Singh and John Davidson

THE MAGIC OF POMEGRANATES FOR HEALTH AND BEAUTY
Natural Remedy Series
JD-Biz Publishing
Dueep J Singh and John Davidson

THE MAGIC OF DRY FRUIT AND SPICES REMEDIES AND RECIPES
Natural Remedy Series
JD-Biz Publishing
Dueep J Singh and John Davidson

THE HEALTH BENEFITS OF TURMERIC CURCUMIN FOR COOKING AND HEALTH
Natural Remedy Series
JD-Biz Publishing
M. Usman and J. Davidson

THE MAGIC OF ALOE VERA
Natural Remedy Series
JD-Biz Publishing
Dueep J Singh and John Davidson

THE MAGIC OF VEGETABLES ANCIENT HEALING REMEDIES AND TIPS
Natural Remedy Series
JD-Biz Publishing
Dueep J Singh and John Davidson

THE HEALTH BENEFITS OF ROSEMARY FOR COOKING AND HEALTH
Natural Remedy Series
JD-Biz Publishing
M. Usman and J. Davidson

THE MAGIC OF PEPPER & PEPPERCORNS FOR COOKING & HEALING
Natural Remedy Series
JD-Biz Publishing
Dueep J Singh and John Davidson

THE MAGIC OF MILK, BUTTER AND CHEESE FOR COOKING & HEALING
Natural Remedy Series
JD-Biz Publishing
Dueep J Singh and John Davidson

THE MAGIC OF CARDAMOMS FOR COOKING AND HEALTH
Health Learning Series
JD-Biz Publishing
Dueep J Singh and John Davidson

THE HEALTH BENEFITS OF BLACK CUMIN FOR COOKING AND HEALTH
Natural Remedy Series
JD-Biz Publishing
M. Usman and J. Davidson

THE MAGIC OF BASIL-TULSI TO HEAL NATURALLY
Health Learning Series
JD-Biz Publishing
Dueep J Singh and John Davidson

THE MAGIC OF SPICES FOR HEALTH AND CUISINE
Natural Remedy Series
JD-Biz Publishing
Dueep J Singh and John Davidson

THE MAGIC OF ROSES FOR COOKING AND BEAUTY
Natural Remedy Series
JD-Biz Publishing
Dueep J Singh and John Davidson

The Miraculous Healing Powers of GINGER
Natural Remedy Series
BEST
Dueep J Singh and John Davidson

The Miracle of HONEY
Natural Remedy Series
JD-Biz Publishing
Dueep J Singh and John Davidson
BEST

Country Life Books

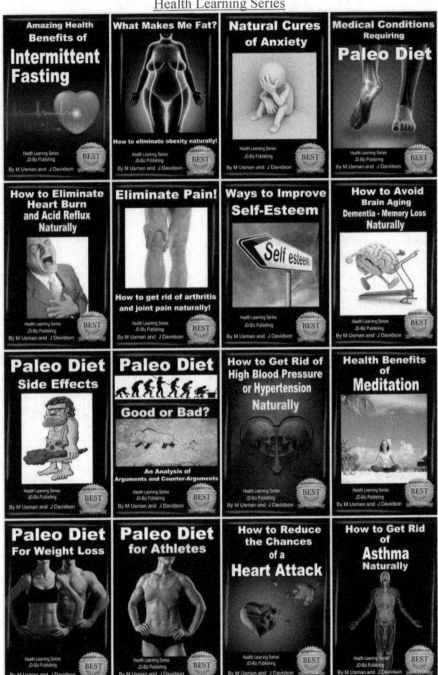

Amazing Animal Book Series

Learn To Draw Series

How to Build and Plan Books

Entrepreneur Book Series

Our books are available at

1. Amazon.com

2. Barnes and Noble

3. Itunes

4. Kobo

5. Smashwords

6. Google Play Books

Publisher

JD-Biz Corp

P O Box 374

Mendon, Utah 84325

http://www.jd-biz.com/

Mendon Cottage Books

P O Box 374, Mendon Utah 84325

CPSIA information can be obtained
at www.ICGtesting.com
Printed in the USA
LVHW081311060320
649214LV00014B/667